MW01179015

With Combo Accompaniment
Arranged by DAVE WOLPE

A Collection of 10 Songs Featuring Vocal Soloist

B♭ Trumpet

Contents

INSTRUMENTATION

Solo Vocalist (SPVM03001)

B♭ Trumpet (SPVM03002)

E♭ Alto Saxophone (SPVM03003)

B♭ Tenor Saxophone (SPVM03004)

Trombone (SPVM03005)

Guitar (SPVM03006)

Bass (SPVM03007)

Drums (SPVM03008)

Piano/Conductor (SPVM03009)

Project Manager: **Pete BarenBregge**
Production Coordinator: **Edmond Randle**
Design & Art Layout: **Lisa Greene Mane**

NICE WORK IF YOU CAN GET IT

Bb Trumpet

Music and Lyrics by
GEORGE GERSHWIN and IRA GERSHWIN
Arranged by DAVE WOLPE

EMBRACEABLE YOU

Music and Lyrics by
GEORGE GERSHWIN and IRA GERSHWIN
Arranged by DAVE WOLPE

Bb Trumpet

4

LOVE IS HERE TO STAY

Bb Trumpet

Music and Lyrics by
GEORGE GERSHWIN and IRA GERSHWIN
Arranged by DAVE WOLPE

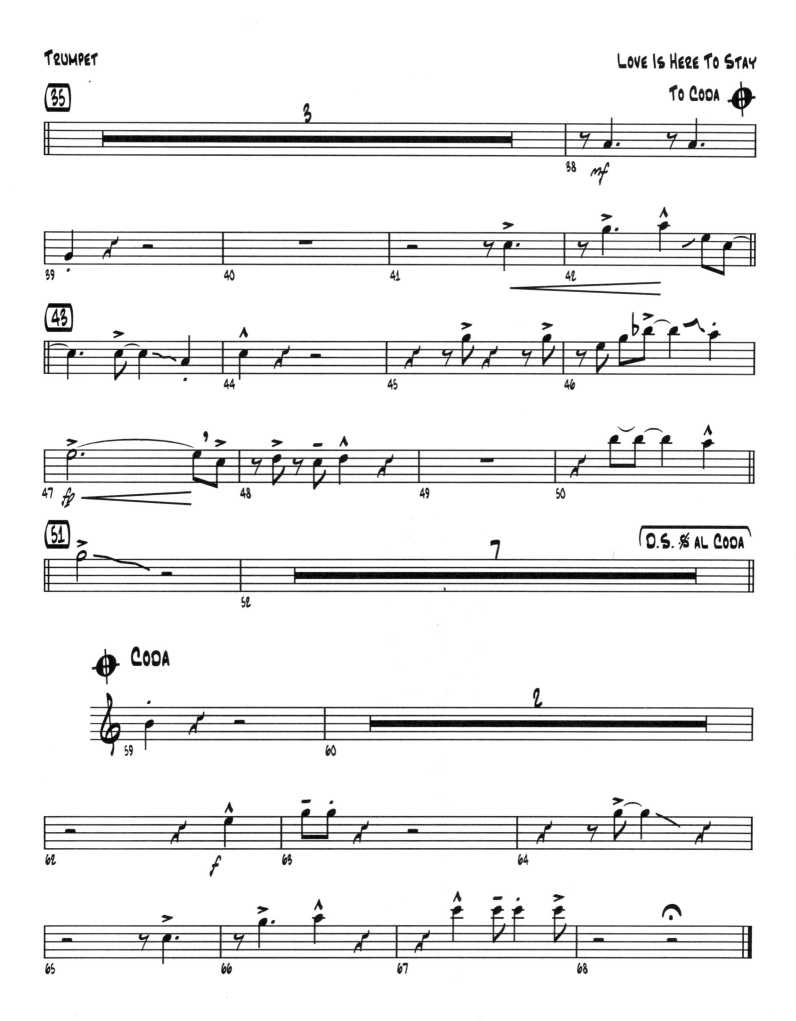

THE MAN I LOVE

Bb Trumpet

Music and Lyrics by
GEORGE GERSHWIN and IRA GERSHWIN
Arranged by DAVE WOLPE

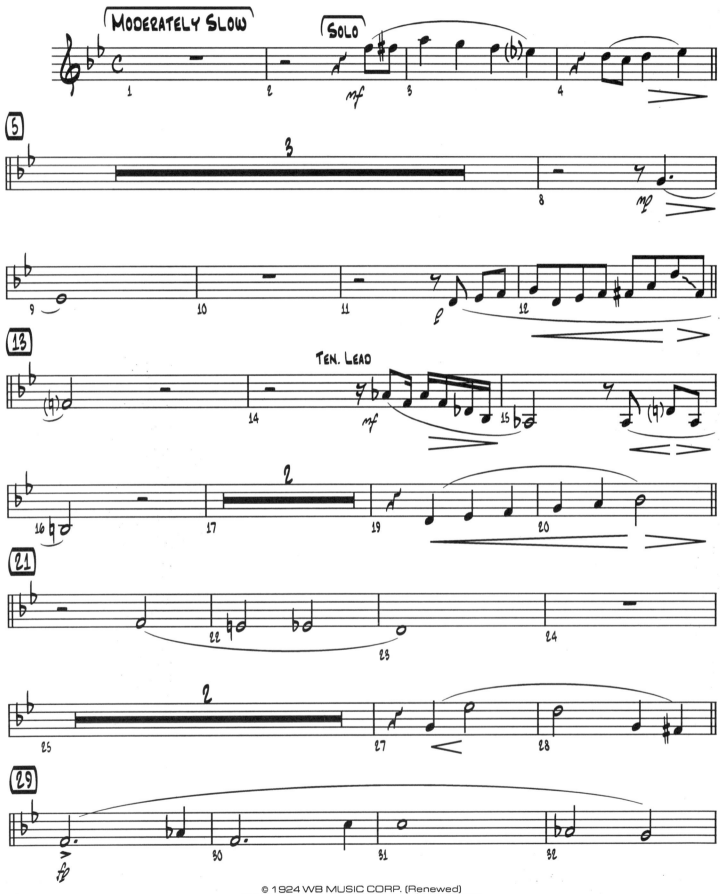

YOU DO SOMETHING TO ME

Bb Trumpet

Words and Music by
COLE PORTER
Arranged By DAVE WOLPE

DO NOTHIN' TILL YOU HEAR FROM ME

Music by DUKE ELLINGTON
Lyric by BOB RUSSELL
Arranged by DAVE WOLPE

Bb Trumpet

THE LADY IS A TRAMP

Words by LORENZ HART
Music by RICHARD RODGERS
Arranged by DAVE WOLPE

Bb Trumpet

HOW LONG HAS THIS BEEN GOING ON?

Music and Lyrics by
GEORGE GERSHWIN and IRA GERSHWIN
Arranged by DAVE WOLPE

Bb Trumpet

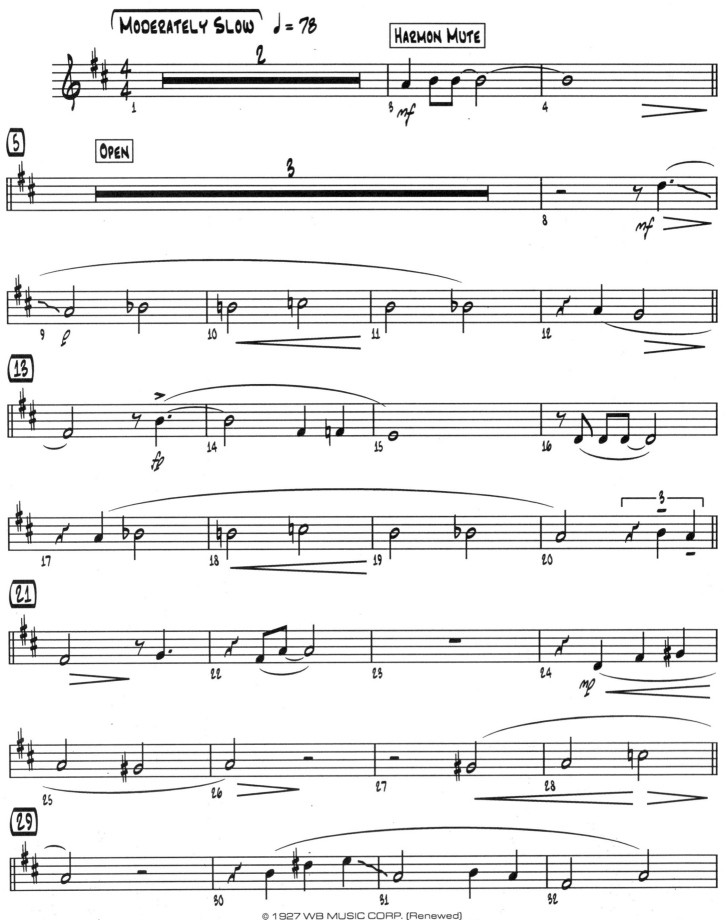

SUMMERTIME

(From PORGY AND BESS ®)

By GEORGE GERSHWIN,
DuBOSE and DOROTHY HEYWARD
and IRA GERSHWIN
Arranged by DAVE WOLPE

Bb Trumpet

MOONLIGHT IN VERMONT

Bb Trumpet

Music by KARL SUESSDORF
Lyric by JOHN BLACKBURN
Arranged by DAVE WOLPE